Where the Red Fern Grows

L-I-T Guide

Literature In Teaching

By Wilson Rawls

A Study Guide for Grades 5 and up
Prepared by Charlotte S. Jaffe and Barbara T. Doherty
Illustrated by Karen Sigler

ISBN 1-56644-022-X

Revised Edition © 1998 Educational Impressions, Inc., Hawthorne, NJ

EDUCATIONAL IMPRESSIONS, INC.
Hawthorne, NJ 07507

Printed in the United States.

Where the Red Fern Grows
Written by Wilson Rawls

STORY SUMMARY

The rugged Ozarks are home to ten-year-old Billy Colman. The log home he shares with his parents and sisters is nestled in a beautiful valley beneath the majestic mountains. It is wonderful hunting country, and Billy longs for two coon hounds to help him fulfill his dream of becoming a hunter. Although his father cannot afford to buy him the dogs, Billy does not give up hope. With the help of his understanding grandfather, Billy decides to earn the fifty dollars needed to buy two hounds by doing odd jobs and saving all that he earns. Although it takes him two years to attain his goal, Billy's hard work and determination finally pay off.

At last the day comes for Billy to meet his dogs. He must travel the long distance from his home to the town depot. In town he must endure the taunts of ''hillbilly'' from the local school children. When he sees the puppies, however, Billy knows that his efforts have been worthwhile.

Billy immediately begins to train his pups, whom he has named Little Ann and Old Dan. Before long the dogs are among the finest hunting teams in the region. They are so good, in fact, that Grandpa decides to enter them in the Championship Coon Hunt; this delights Billy. Billy, Grandpa, and Papa help mother prepare things at home and then set off for the campground where the contest is to be held. The coon hunt is filled with adventure and peril—Grandpa suffers an injury and the dogs nearly freeze to death; nevertheless, Billy manages to come home with two medals: a silver and a gold. Little Ann wins the silver for best-looking hound, and the two dogs win the gold for the best team.

Upon returning home, the glory of victory is short lived. Old Dan is killed as the result of a vicious fight with a bobcat, and a mourning Little Ann dies soon after of a broken heart. Billy is heartbroken, but his grief subsides when he sees that a beautiful red fern is growing on the spot where they were buried. According to an old Indian legend, a red fern can only be planted by an angel; therefore, to Billy, the spot will always be blessed. The story ends as Billy and his family leave the Ozark Mountains to begin a new life in town.

Meet the Author
Wilson Rawls

Wilson Rawls was born in 1913 on the family farm in a very rural area of the Ozarks in the heart of Cherokee country. His only companion was his blue tick hound. Wilson did not attend school. From his mother, he learned to read and write using story books that she had ordered from catalogs.

At about age ten he was given a copy of *The Call of the Wild,* by Jack London. This was the first book he ever owned; he kept it with him wherever he went! It made such an impression on him that he decided at an early age to become a writer.

At first he wrote in the dirt of the country roads and in the sand along the river. He practiced describing the things that he knew best—the things around the farm. When his family moved to Muskogee, Oklahoma, Wilson at last was able to attend school. He enrolled in the high school there and finally had access to books and writing materials.

Wilson was a teenager during the Depression. He left home and wandered throughout the country looking for work. Wherever he wandered, however, he kept writing. He saved all of his ideas and kept them safely stored. One of the reasons that he never shared his writings was that he never learned grammar, spelling, or punctuation. He was ashamed that he could not use these things correctly. After he married, his wife encouraged him by correcting his work and helping him master the things he did not know.

Where the Red Fern Grows was based largely on his own childhood. It was first published in 1961. In 1974 it was made into a movie.

Wilson Rawls and his wife never had any children. He visited schools often and spoke to students about his books. He encouraged them never to give up in their attempt to fulfill their dreams. Wilson Rawls died in 1984 after a lengthy illness.

Pre-Reading Activity
Where in the U.S.A. Are They?

Because this story is based on his own boyhood memories, Wilson Rawls set *Where the Red Fern Grows* in rural Oklahoma during the 1930's. The closest city or town to the Colman farm was Tahlequah, Oklahoma. In Chapter I the narrator also mentioned the Snake River Valley in Idaho. This is the area where Mr. and Mrs. Rawls settled after they were married.

The following map shows Oklahoma and the surrounding states.

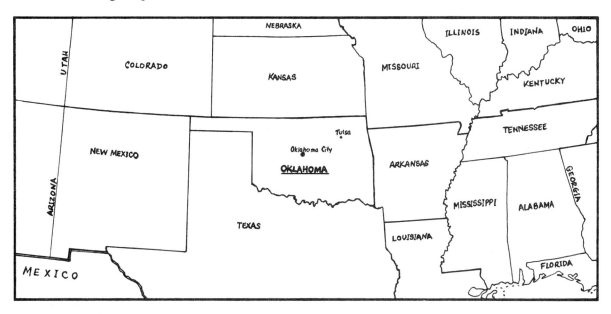

Complete the following activities with your cooperative-learning group.

1. Locate and add to the map the Ozark Mountains, which are partly in Oklahoma. In what other state(s) are they?

_____

2. Locate and add to the map Tahlequah.

3. Find Oklahoma on a map of the U.S.A. Is it north, south, east, or west of your state?_____

4. Compare Oklahoma to your state in size. _____

5. Find Idaho on a map of the U.S.A. Compare it to Oklahoma. Are there any similarities?

_____

6. Find out the following information about Oklahoma:

Nickname: _____

Capital: _____

Major Products and Industries: _____

_____

Vocabulary
Chapters One and Two

Use the words in the box to solve the crossword puzzle. Not all of the words will be used.

alley	aromatic	bore	bribery	Cherokee	crosscut
crude	darted	dormant	foothills	gnaw	grieve
hedge	mass	muzzle	nestled	pen	reared
romp	sanitation	scald	snarl	turpentine	whine

Across

1. Tribe of Native Americans now settled in Oklahoma.
3. To wear away by repeated nibbling.
5. Moved swiftly.
7. Make a hole through.
8. To confine to an enclosure.
9. Fragrant.
11. Lying sheltered.
13. Growl viciously.
15. Rough; not carefully made.
17. Process of keeping things free from health hazards.

Down

2. Row of shrubs.
3. To experience sorrow.
4. To utter a troubled cry.
6. Rose up on its hind legs.
7. Giving something to influence or persuade.
10. An amount of something that clings together.
12. Mixture of oil and resin.
14. At rest.
16. To play in a rough, noisy way.

Comprehension and Discussion Questions
Chapter One

Answer the following questions in complete sentence form. Give examples from the story to support your response.

1. Why didn't the narrator try to make the hound his own?

_____

_____

_____

_____

2. Why did the narrator think that something drastic had happened to this dog?

_____

_____

_____

_____

3. Where did the narrator think the dog was trying to go? Do you agree? Why or why not?

_____

_____

_____

_____

4. Can you predict the significance of the gold and silver cups? What might the narrator's boyhood memories be?

_____

_____

_____

_____

Comprehension and Discussion Questions
Chapter Two

Answer the following questions in complete sentence form. Give examples from the story to support your response.

1. Why was Billy's family allowed to live on Cherokee land?

_____

_____

_____

_____

2. Why did Billy's father offer to get Billy a collie? How did Billy react?

_____

_____

_____

_____

3. Evaluate the success of Billy's father's decision to get Billy the traps.

_____

_____

_____

_____

4. Pretend to be Billy's mom or dad. Write an entry in your diary describing how you felt when Billy begged for the hounds.

_____

_____

_____

_____

Vocabulary
Chapters Three and Four

Alphabetize the words or phrases in the box. Then define them according to their use in the story.

festered	depot	pangs	hoeing	astonishment
hillbilly	dumbfounded	crawfish	mulled	haunches
eaves	caloused	provisions	residential	gawked
sorghum	quavering	gunny sack	flailing	

Headliners

Use the vocabulary words (or forms of the words) from the first part of this activity to create three headlines. The topics may vary. Try to use more than one vocabulary word per headline.

Example: **Gunny Sacks of Provisions Arrive at Depot**

Comprehension and Discussion Questions
Chapter Three

Answer the following questions in complete sentence form. Give examples from the story to support your response.

1. What did Billy find at the fisherman's camp? How important was it to him?

_____

_____

_____

_____

2. How did Billy earn his money?

_____

_____

_____

_____

3. Grandpa advised Billy not to say anything about the money to his father. Why? Judge whether Grandpa was right to give this advice.

_____

_____

_____

_____

4. Write a brief character sketch of Billy based upon what you learned in this chapter.

_____

_____

_____

_____

Comprehension and Discussion Questions
Chapter Four

Answer the following questions in complete sentence form. Give examples from the story to support your response.

1. Why did Grandpa give Billy ten dollars?

_____

_____

_____

_____

2. What did Billy see for the first time when he looked in the storefront window? What did he realize?

_____

_____

_____

_____

3. Why didn't Billy realize that the red brick building was a school?

_____

_____

_____

_____

4. How do you think Billy felt after his experiences in Tahlequah? Have you ever had a similar experience?

_____

_____

_____

_____

Vocabulary
Chapters Five and Six

Use the words in the box to complete the sentences below. You may need to use your dictionary. Not all of the words will be used.

bawl	hampered	prowled	trance
cautious	iodine	querying	unravel
chuckling	mumbling	shucks	ventured
gawked	muster	sober	vicious

1. John warned Jeff to be _____ when handling the dangerous chemicals.

2. The _____ stung when applied to the cut.

3. The small boy tried to _____ up the courage to volunteer for the play.

4. The downed trees _____ the driver's passage.

5. When the girls saw their favorite actor, they stood and _____ at him.

6. They tried not to laugh at his silly outfit, but they couldn't help _____.

7. The puppy gave out such a loud _____ that he could be heard next door.

8. Jack removed the _____ from the corn.

9. Mr. Jones was in a very serious mood; he spoke in a _____ tone.

10. Janet was so absorbed in her task that she seemed to be in a _____.

11. Bob had a _____ look when he asked her to repeat the question.

12. Melissa was afraid to drive in the snow, but she _____ out anyway.

13. The lion _____ the jungle in search of prey.

14. Because she was _____, her mother couldn't understand her.

Another Way of Saying It
Choose six of the above sentences. Rewrite each of them using a synonym for the vocabulary word used in the first part of this activity.

Example: John warned Jeff to be **careful** when handling the dangerous chemicals.

Comprehension and Discussion Questions
Chapter Five

Answer the following questions in complete sentence form. Give examples from the story to support your response.

1. Judge Billy's decision to fight ''Freckle-face.''

_____

_____

_____

_____

2. How did Billy's opinion of marshals change? Why?

_____

_____

_____

_____

3. Compare and contrast the two pups.

_____

_____

_____

_____

4. How do you think Billy felt now that he had his pups?

_____

_____

_____

_____

Comprehension and Discussion Questions
Chapter Six

Answer the following questions in complete sentence form. Give examples from the story to support your response.

1. Why did Billy stop and wait at the campground?

_____

_____

_____

_____

2. How did Billy decide on the names for the puppies? Evaluate his method and judge his choice of names.

_____

_____

_____

_____

3. How did Billy's parents and sisters react? Did their reactions surprise you? Explain.

_____

_____

_____

_____

4. Judge Papa's belief that the family should move to town one day.

_____

_____

_____

_____

Vocabulary
Chapters Seven and Eight

Match the vocabulary words on the left to the definitions on the right. Place the correct letter on each line.

_____ 1. alert

_____ 2. anxious

_____ 3. bay

_____ 4. bewildered

_____ 5. cease

_____ 6. den

_____ 7. domain

_____ 8. gleam

_____ 9. gouge

_____ 10. hover

_____ 11. limber

_____ 12. peculiarity

_____ 13. persistence

_____ 14. obstacle

_____ 15. shed

_____ 16. stir

_____ 17. wiley

_____ 18. woe

A. a wild animal's shelter

B. to move to and fro near a place

C. steadfastness; perseverance

D. bending easily

E. eager; impatiently waiting

F. watchful

G. to be active or busy

H. territory over which control is exercised

I. small structure for storage

J. crafty; sly; cunning

K. stop

L. sorrow; grief

M. confused

N. something in way of progress or achievement

O. to cut holes or grooves in

P. to emit a glow

Q. distinguishing characteristic; oddity

R. to bark with long, deep tones

Choose any three vocabulary words from the first part of this activity. Write an original sentence for each.

_____

_____

_____

_____

_____

Comprehension and Discussion Questions
Chapter Seven

Answer the following questions in complete sentence form. Give examples from the story to support your response.

1. According to Grandpa, what peculiarity does a raccoon have that would make his plan work?

_____

_____

_____

_____

2. What evidence is there that Billy's dog Dan will be a good coon hound?

_____

_____

_____

_____

3. Why was Billy told not to trap any more raccoons?

_____

_____

_____

_____

4. Describe how Billy trained his pups to follow the scent of a raccoon.

_____

_____

_____

_____

Comprehension and Discussion Questions
Chapter Eight

Answer the following questions in complete sentence form. Give examples from the story to support your response.

1. What preparations did Billy make for the first night of hunting?

_____

_____

_____

_____

2. Billy noticed a change in his relationship with his father. Describe that change.

_____

_____

_____

_____

3. What did the dogs do that made Billy know that his talk to them had been a success?

_____

_____

_____

_____

4. Explain the following statement: ''After Papa left, things were a little different. The tree didn't look as big, and my ax wasn't as heavy.''

_____

_____

_____

_____

Vocabulary
Chapters Nine and Ten

Alphabetize the vocabulary words in the box below. Then use your dictionary to define the words according to their use in the story.

loft	belligerent	hysterical	feat	abounded
flint	peroxide	slough	riffle	salve
eerie	predicament	brutal	winced	nuzzling
coaxed	miraculous	throbbed	sockets	hacking

Thanks, Grandpa

Pretend you are Billy. Now that you have successfully trained your dogs, you want to write a letter to Grandpa expressing how you feel. Use at least eight of the vocabulary words from the first part of this activity in your letter.

Comprehension and Discussion Questions
Chapter Nine

Answer the following questions in complete sentence form. Give examples from the story to support your response.

1. Why was Billy upset at the beginning of this chapter?

_____

_____

_____

_____

2. Describe Grandpa's plan. How did Billy know that he was serious?

_____

_____

_____

_____

3. Felling the tree caused Billy to have mixed emotions. Why?

_____

_____

_____

_____

4. Do you think that Billy is religious? Give evidence to support your opinion.

_____

_____

_____

_____

Comprehension and Discussion Questions
Chapter Ten

Answer the following questions in complete sentence form. Give examples from the story to support your response.

1. Judge Billy's way of dealing with the teasing of the coon hunters.

_____

_____

_____

_____

2. Why, do you think, was Billy given complete freedom from work during the fur season?

_____

_____

_____

_____

3. According to Billy, how did the raccoon caught in the muskrat den get so smart?

_____

_____

_____

_____

4. Billy thought that his dogs were "the greatest." Give at least two examples from this chapter of this greatness.

_____

_____

_____

_____

Vocabulary
Chapters Eleven and Twelve

Match the vocabulary words on the left to the definitions on the right. Place the correct letter on each line.

_____ 1. eddy		A.	a tube that carries blood from the heart
_____ 2. cease		B.	to move nervously
_____ 3. rile		C.	rolling about clumsily
_____ 4. fidget		D.	a rapid to-and-fro movement
_____ 5. underbrush		E.	to come up with too low a figure
_____ 6. stomp		F.	a current moving in a circle
_____ 7. vibration		G.	sly, cunning look
_____ 8. underestimate		H.	small shrubs and trees
_____ 9. ventilating		I.	a building where lumber is cut
_____ 10. artery		J.	to stop
_____ 11. begrudgingly		K.	circulating air to freshen
_____ 12. bawling		L.	to make angry; to irritate
_____ 13. leer		M.	a place where water is not deep
_____ 14. maneuver		N.	with reluctance
_____ 15. surpass		O.	to tread on; to trample
_____ 16. sawmill		P.	movement requiring skill
_____ 17. shallows		Q.	weeping loudly
_____ 18. wallowing		R.	to do better than

Choose any three vocabulary words from the first part of this activity. Write an original sentence for each.

_____

_____

_____

_____

Comprehension and Discussion Questions
Chapter Eleven

Answer the following questions in complete sentence form. Give examples from the story to support your response.

1. Evaluate Billy's decision to go hunting on such a "dark, slick night." List the pros and cons.

_____

_____

_____

_____

2. How did Billy know that Little Ann was in trouble? Describe her predicament.

_____

_____

_____

_____

3. How did Billy's strong faith lead him to a solution to his problem?

_____

_____

_____

_____

4. What would you have done if you had been in Billy's situation?

_____

_____

_____

_____

Comprehension and Discussion Questions
Chapter Twelve

Answer the following questions in complete sentence form. Give examples from the story to support your response.

1. Why, do you think, did Grandpa agree to the bet? Would you have made the bet? Why or why not?

_____

_____

_____

_____

2. Characterize Rubin and Rainie. According to Mother, what was the reason for their meanness? Do you think this should have excused their behavior?

_____

_____

_____

_____

3. How did the ghost coon get his name?

_____

_____

_____

_____

4. Predict whether or not the ghost coon was in the tree at the end of the chapter. Support your opinion.

_____

_____

_____

_____

Vocabulary
Chapters Thirteen and Fourteen

For each sentence circle the most appropriate definition for the word printed in bold as it is used in the sentence. Use your dictionary to help you. The first has been done for you.

1. Papa placed the **halter** around the mule's neck.

    blouse   (rope)   chain   saddle

2. The teacher's **droning** voice nearly put the students to sleep.

    harsh   soft   monotonous   irritating

3. The winners of the race were **jubilant.**

    relieved   content   tired   joyful

4. When they defeated their rivals, the team members **gloated.**

    felt great relief   felt malicious delight   felt embarrassed   felt great pride

5. **Solemn** organ music was played during the memorial service.

    modern   soft   serious   lively

6. Their disagreement caused quite a **commotion** in the room.

    discussion   disturbance   exchange   gathering

7. Getting **astraddle** of Little Ann, Billy pried her jaws apart.

    close to   underneath   next to   with a leg on each side

8. Sara **blurted** out the secret before I could stop her.

    uttered impulsively   said slowly   shouted   stuttered

9. The dog was **nipping** the man's leg.

    licking   biting   shaking   circling

10. He kept his emotions **pent up**.

    repressed   in the open   expressed   unimportant

11. The soldiers faced little **resistance** from the enemy.

    suffering   help   respect   opposition

12. Do you believe in the **existence** of ghosts?

    being   nearness   frightfulness   transparency

Comprehension and Discussion Questions
Chapter Thirteen

Answer the following questions in complete sentence form. Give examples from the story to support your response.

1. Explain Rubin's reasons for accusing Billy of being crazy and calling him chicken livered.

_____

_____

_____

_____

2. Why did Rubin threaten, "If you say one word to your Grandpa about this, I'll catch you hunting some night and take my knife to you"?

_____

_____

_____

_____

3. How did Billy's ax cause a tragedy? Could this tragedy have been prevented? Explain.

_____

_____

_____

_____

4. In what way did the small bouquet of flowers help to lift Billy's spirits?

_____

_____

_____

_____

Comprehension and Discussion Questions
Chapter Fourteen

Answer the following questions in complete sentence form. Give examples from the story to support your response.

1. Why did Grandpa think that he was to blame for Rubin's death? Do you think that he should bear some of the responsibility? Explain your views.

_____

_____

_____

_____

2. What did Grandpa want to discuss with Billy besides Rubin's death?

_____

_____

_____

_____

3. Explain the following simile: "Grandpa flew out of gear like a Model-T Ford."

_____

_____

_____

_____

4. Why was Billy hesitant about taking his ax? Judge his decision to take it.

_____

_____

_____

_____

Vocabulary
Chapters Fifteen and Sixteen

Use your dictionary to define the following words as they were used in the chapter.

1. bawling

2. bayou

3. bristle

4. current

5. disqualified

6. eliminated

7. flint

8. gauge

9. glistened

10. glossy

11. runoff

12. snuff

13. spectacles

14. squall

15. stride

16. superstition

17. tension

18. twittering

Be a Song Writer

In Chapter Fifteen, Billy sang a verse of a song that he created. Complete the song by writing more verses. Use at least six vocabulary words from the first part of this activity.

You can swim the river, Old Mister Ringtail,
And play your tricks out one by one.
It won't do any good, Old Mister Ringtail,
My Little Ann knows every one.

Comprehension and Discussion Questions
Chapter Fifteen

Answer the following questions in complete sentence form. Give examples from the story to support your response.

1. Grandpa characterized Billy's dogs as being strange. Give examples of their strangeness.

_____

_____

_____

_____

2. What did Grandpa do that made Billy feel proud?

_____

_____

_____

_____

3. Describe the superstition that worried Billy. Tell about a superstition that worries you.

_____

_____

_____

_____

4. What caused Bily to cry? Have you ever cried for happiness? Relate your experience.

_____

_____

_____

_____

Comprehension and Discussion Questions
Chapter Sixteen

Answer the following questions in complete sentence form. Give examples from the story to support your response.

1. What caused the judge to say, "I've been hunting coons and judging coon hunts for forty years, but I've never seen anything like that"?

_____

_____

_____

_____

2. Why did Grandpa say, "We've got to get one more coon, even if I have to tree it myself"?

_____

_____

_____

_____

3. Guess why the hunters were rooting for Billy to win the jackpot.

_____

_____

_____

_____

4. How did the dogs show their love for one another?

_____

_____

_____

_____

Vocabulary
Chapters Seventeen and Eighteen

Use the following vocabulary words in original sentences that describe a story happening.

1. cobbler

2. despair

3. engrave

4. haggard

5. harmony

6. harnessing

7. instinct

8. leeward

9. mackinaw

10. snag

11. stampede

12. unconscious

13. wedges

Read All About It

Pretend that you are a reporter for the *Ozark Gazette*. Write an account of the Championship Hunt. Use at least six of the vocabulary words from the first part of this activity in your story.

Comprehension and Discussion Questions
Chapter Seventeen

Answer the following questions in complete sentence form. Give examples from the story to support your response.

1. How did Billy convince Papa not to return to camp during the storm? Judge Papa's decision to continue.

_____

_____

_____

_____

2. How did Billy get Little Ann to come to him?

_____

_____

_____

_____

3. Describe Grandpa's misfortune.

_____

_____

_____

_____

4. What did the dogs do when Billy pointed in the direction the coon had taken? Why did this astonish the judge?

_____

_____

_____

_____

Comprehension and Discussion Questions
Chapter Eighteen

Answer the following questions in complete sentence form. Give examples from the story to support your response.

1. Why was Grandpa lucky after all?

_____

_____

_____

_____

2. Why did Mr. Benson's description of the dogs cause Billy great pain?

_____

_____

_____

_____

3. Characterize the other hunters. Give reasons for your opinion.

_____

_____

_____

_____

4. What made Billy decide not to have the engraving done on the championship cup?

_____

_____

_____

_____

Vocabulary
Chapters Nineteen and Twenty

Read each clue and find the answers in the box. Then use the letters above the numbered spaces to decipher the secret message.

> entrails   fangs   sandstone   ghastly
>
> gristle   ledge   painstaking   peroxide   petrified
>
> pitiful   vibration   sacred   foliage   shimmering
>
> spewing   predatory   bellow   unblinking

1. roar; shout in a deep voice   __ __ __ __ __ __
    1   3   4

2. body's internal organs   __ __ __ __ __ __ __ __
     2

3. long teeth   __ __ __ __ __
    28

4. plant leaves   __ __ __ __ __ __ __
   7   6

5. rapid movement   __ __ __ __ __ __ __ __ __
   8   17   21

6. cartilage; a tough tissue in meat   __ __ __ __ __ __ __
     24   9

7. causing terror   __ __ __ __ __ __ __
    10   5

8. narrow shelf   __ __ __ __ __
  11

9. arousing sorrow   __ __ __ __ __ __ __
   12 13   15

10. sedimentary rock   __ __ __ __ __ __ __ __ __
    18   14   19 16

11. holy   __ __ __ __ __ __
   20   22

12. an antiseptic   __ __ __ __ __ __ __ __
    23   25

13. preying on other animals   __ __ __ __ __ __ __ __ __
    26 27

1   2   3   4   5   6   7   8   9   10   11   12   13   14   15   16

__ __ __ __ __   __ __ __ __ __   __ __ __ __ __ __

17   18   19   20   21   22   23   24   25   26   27   28

__ __ __   __ __ __   __ __ __   __ __ __

Comprehension and Discussion Questions
Chapter Nineteen

Answer the following questions in complete sentence form. Give examples from the story to support your response.

1. Billy was afraid and wanted to leave the area. Why wouldn't Old Dan leave?

_____

_____

_____

_____

2. What did Billy do to save the lives of his dogs? What did the dogs do to save Billy's life?

_____

_____

_____

_____

3. Why did Billy choose the hillside as a burial spot for Old Dan?

_____

_____

_____

_____

4. In the previous chapter, Mama said that her prayers had been answered. In this chapter we found out what she meant. Explain.

_____

_____

_____

_____

Comprehension and Discussion Questions
Chapter Twenty

Answer the following questions in complete sentence form. Give examples from the story to support your response.

1. What was the mood of the family on moving day? Why did they feel that way?

_____

_____

_____

_____

2. What was special about finding a red fern growing on the dogs' graves?

_____

_____

_____

_____

3. Choose one of the characters. As that character, describe the mixed feelings you had as you pulled away from your home.

_____

_____

_____

_____

4. What valuable lessons did you learn from reading this story?

_____

_____

_____

_____

Spotlight Literary Skill
Mood

Mood is the feeling or effect that is created by the author's words. Settings, actions, characterizations and descriptions can all be written to convey certain moods. Read the following story selections and think about how the passages make you feel.

On the line below each selection, describe the mood that the author has created:

1. "Freckle-face pulled the ear of my little girl pup. I heard her painful cry. That was too much. I hadn't worked two long years for my pups to have some freckle-face punk pull their ears."

_____

2. "Then I saw something else. The sun was just right, and the plate glass was a perfect mirror. I saw the full reflection of myself for the first time in my life."

_____

3. "I don't know where they came from, but like chicken coming home to roost, they flocked around me. Some were a little bigger, some smaller. They ganged around me screaming and yelling. They started clapping their hands and chanting, 'The dog-boy has come to town. The dog-boy has come to town.' "

_____

4. "I was scared and I called to him. I wanted to get away from there . . . . Then I saw them—two burning, yellow eyes—staring at me from the shadowy foliage of the tree. I stopped, petrified with fear . . . . Again the silence closed in."

_____

5. "There was a celebration in our home that night. To me it was like a second Christmas."

_____

Spotlight Literary Skill
Cause and Effect

Sometimes a certain event or action brings about another event or action. This is what is meant by **cause and effect.** Read the following: "Because it was raining, we couldn't play baseball." The fact that it was raining is the cause. The fact that we couldn't play baseball is the effect. In other words, it was the fact that it was raining that caused us not to play baseball.

Match the causes in the column on the left with the effects in the column on the right. Place the correct letter on each line.

CAUSES	EFFECTS
____ 1. Billy's mother was part Cherokee.	A. Billy saved all of his money for two years.
____ 2. Billy wanted to buy two hound dogs.	B. The pup cried.
____ 3. The price of dogs dropped.	C. The family was given a plot of land in a valley of the Ozarks.
____ 4. A boy pulled the girl pup's ears.	D. Grandpa learned a lot about raccoons' habits.
____ 5. The marshal was kind to Billy.	E. Billy felt grown-up.
____ 6. The city was very crowded.	F. Billy's mom wanted to move to the city.
____ 7. There were no schools near Billy's home.	G. Billy thought his dogs were dead.
____ 8. Grandpa had watched his pet raccoon.	H. Billy no longer feared marshals.
____ 9. Grandpa poured coffee for Billy.	I. Billy had ten dollars to spend on presents.
____ 10. Mr. Benson said that the dogs were frozen solid.	J. Billy preferred to live in the country.

Spotlight Literary Skill
Flashback

Flashback is a literary technique in which the author interrupts the current sequence of time to describe events that happened earlier. In *Where the Red Fern Grows*, Wilson Rawls starts his story when Billy is a grown man and he flashes back to Billy's life as a boy growing up in the Ozarks. At the very end of the book Mr. Rawls returns to the present time.

If you could interview the grown-up Billy, what questions would you ask him about his life after the story ends? Perhaps you wonder why he never returned to visit his childhood home.

Make a list of ten questions. Then exchange with a classmate to create possible answers.

1

2

3

4

5

6

7

8

9

10

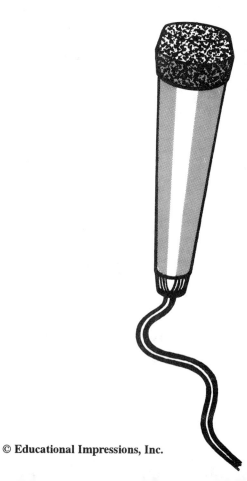

Spotlight Literary Skill
Colorful Language

The use of personification, similes, and other forms of figurative language allows us to express our ideas with more interest and variety. They make our language more *colorful!*

PERSONIFICATION

Personification is when an author or speaker gives human characteristics, actions, or feelings to animals, non-living objects, events, or abstract ideas.

Example: The flowers danced happily in the meadow.

SIMILES

A **simile** uses the word ''like'' or the word ''as'' to compare two unlike things.

Example: He is as sly as a fox.

Find examples of figurative language in the story. Write your examples and the page numbers on which you found them. Tell whether each is personification, simile or other form of figurative language.

_____

_____

_____

_____

_____

_____

_____

_____

_____

_____

Choose one of the above examples and illustrate it.

Cooperative Learning Activity
Eulogy to a Friend

*"You were worth it, old friend,
and a thousand times over."*

A **eulogy** is a speech or writing in praise of someone who has died. The above words were voiced by Billy as he buried Old Dan. Try to recall story events that revealed Billy's love for his dog. Use them to develop Billy's statement into a eulogy. Work with your cooperative learning group. When you have completed your work, compare your eulogy orally with those of the other classroom groups.

Eulogy for Old Dan

_____

_____

_____

_____

_____

_____

_____

Post Reading Activities

1. Research the sport of hunting. Discuss game laws, types of hunting, and necessary equipment. Some find hunting a satisfying sport. Others feel it is wrong to hunt. How do you feel about it?

2. Obtain books from your school or public library containing Native American legends. Read some to your classmates. Discuss these and legends from other countries.

3. Imagine that you are Billy. Write a diary of your daily thoughts, hopes, and fears. Record your impressions of other story characters.

4. What did you learn about family relationships from this story?

5. Separate into small cooperative-learning groups. Each group will choose a chapter or section of the book to dramatize.

6. Create a poster to encourage other students in your school to read *Where the Red Fern Grows*. Place your poster in the hallway or library of your school.

7. In this story Billy encountered many problems. Select one problem and tell how you would have handled it differently.

8. Construct a roller movie to show your favorite parts of the book.

9. In the story Billy received a gold cup, but he chose not to have it engraved. Design your own award for Billy. Inscribe it with a message that tells why you think he deserved to win it.

10. An **acrostic** is a type of poem developed from the name of a person, place, or thing or from a series of letters. The name is written in a vertical (up and down) line. Usually the lines tell something about the word or words being spelled. Create an acrostic poem of your own. Use one of the following titles as the basis of your poem or choose one of your own: Raccoons, Ozarks, Hunting, Hound Dogs, Billy Colman, Old Dan, Little Ann, Grandpa, or Rural Life. The theme should relate in some way to *Where the Red Fern Grows*.

Crossword Puzzle
Where the Red Fern Grows

See how much you remember about *Where the Red Fern Grows*. Have fun!

Across

2. Billy had ___ sisters.
7. Story is told from his point of view.
8. Grandpa injured this.
11. Upland region of the south central U.S.A.
12. Describes the water Little Ann was rescued from by Billy.
13. He accidentally killed himself on Billy's ax.
16. Billy went to the depot here to get his hound dogs.
17. Saved Billy from being beaten by boys in town.
20. Billy saw his reflection in a store ___.
22. Name of Billy's female dog.
23. Pertaining to the country as opposed to the city.
26. One grew on the spot where Billy's dogs were buried. (2 words)
28. At first Billy didn't realize the red brick building was one.
32. Old Dan was killed fighting one.
33. The Colman family moved there at the end of the novel.
34. According to legend, a red fern must be planted by one.
35. Medal won by Little Ann for best-looking dog.

Down

1. To cut or knock down.
3. The town boys taunted Billy by calling him this.
4. Author's first name.
5. Name of Billy's male dog.
6. Author's last name.
9. Grandpa and Billy built one to fool the coon into thinking a man was there.
10. State where Billy's dog came from. (postal abbreviation).
14. The belief that it is bad luck to hear two screech owls is this.
15. They owned the land the Colman family lived on.
16. 27 Down kept getting caught in one.
18. "Grandpa flew out of gear like a Model-T Ford" is one.
19. He entered Billy's dogs in the championship coon hunt.
21. State in which the novel is set.
24. What "Old Mister Ringtail" referred to in Billy's verse.
25. Little Ann died of a "broken" one.
27. The Colmans' house cat.
29. The Colmans' home was made of these.
30. Medal won by Little Ann and Old Dan for best team.
31. Billy saved for ___ years to buy his dogs.

Glossary of Literary Terms

Alliteration: A repetition of initial, or beginning, sounds in two or more consecutive or neighboring words.

Analogy: A comparison based upon the resemblance in some particular ways between things that are otherwise unlike.

Anecdote: A short account of an interesting, amusing, or biographical occurrence.

Anticlimax: An event that is less important than what occurred before it.

Archaic language: Language that was once common in a particular historic period but which is no longer commonly used.

Cause and effect: The relationship in which one condition brings about another condition as a direct result. The result, or consequence, is called the effect.

Character development: The ways in which the author shows how a character changes as the story proceeds.

Characterization: The method used by the author to give readers information about a character; a description or representation of a person's qualities or peculiarities.

Classify: To arrange according to a category or trait.

Climax: The moment when the action in a story reaches its greatest conflict.

Compare and contrast: To examine the likenesses and differences of two people, ideas or things. (*Contrast* always emphasizes differences. *Compare* may focus on likenesses alone or on likenesses and differences.)

Conflict: The main source of drama and tension in a literary work; the discord between persons or forces that brings about dramatic action.

Connotation: Something suggested or implied, not actually stated.

Description: An account that gives the reader a mental image or picture of something.

Dialect: A form of language used in a certain geographic region; it is distinguished from the standard form of the language by pronunciation, grammar, and/or vocabulary.

Dialogue (dialog): The parts of a literary work that represent conversation.

Fact: A piece of information that can be proven or verified.

Figurative language: Description of one thing in terms usually used for something else. Simile and metaphor are examples of figurative language.

Flashback: The insertion of an earlier event into the normal chronological sequence of a narrative.

Foreshadowing: The use of clues to give readers a hint of events that will occur later on.

Historical fiction: Fiction represented in a setting true to the history of the time in which the story takes place.

Imagery: Language that appeals to the senses; the use of figures of speech or vivid descriptions to produce mental images.

Irony: The use of words to express the opposite of their literal meaning.

Legend: A story handed down from earlier times; its truth is popularly accepted but cannot be verified.

Limerick: A humorous five-lined poem with a specific form: aabba. Lines 1, 2, and 5 are longer than lines 3 and 4.

Metaphor: A figure of speech that compares two unlike things without the use of like or as.

Mood: The feeling that the author creates for the reader.

Motivation: The reasons for the behavior of a character.

Narrative: The type of writing that tells a story.

Narrator: The character who tells the story.

Opinion: A personal point of view or belief.

Parody: Writing that ridicules or imitates something more serious.

Personification: A figure of speech in which an inanimate object or an abstract idea is given human characteristics.

Play: A literary work that is written in dialogue form and that is usually performed before an audience.

Plot: The arrangement or sequence of events in a story.

Point of view: The perspective from which a story is told.

Protagonist: The main character.

Pun: A play on words that are similar in sound but different in meaning.

Realistic fiction: True-to-life fiction; people, places, and happenings are similar to those in real life.

Resolution: The part of the plot from the climax to the ending where the main dramatic conflict is worked out.

Satire: A literary work that pokes fun at individual or societal weaknesses.

Sequencing: The placement of story elements in the order of their occurrence.

Setting: The time and place in which the story occurs.

Simile: A figure of speech that uses *like* or *as* to compare two unlike things.

Stereotype: A character whose personality traits represent a group rather than an individual.

Suspense: Quality that causes readers to wonder what will happen next.

Symbolism: The use of a thing, character, object, or idea to represent something else.

Synonyms: Words that are very similar in meaning.

Tall tale: An exaggerated story detailing unbelievable events.

Theme: The main idea of a literary work; the message the author wants to communicate, sometimes expressed as a generalization about life.

Tone: The quality or feeling conveyed by the work; the author's style or manner of expression.

ANSWERS

Chapters One and Two: Vocabulary

Across

1. Cherokee
3. gnaw
5. darted
7. bore
8. pen
9. aromatic
11. nestled
13. snarl
15. crude
17. sanitation

Down

2. hedge
3. grieve
4. whine
6. reared
7. bribery
10. mass
12. turpentine
14. dormant
16. romp

Chapter One: Comprehension and Discussion Questions (Answers may vary.)

1. He knew that it was a hunting dog and that it would not be happy in the city. "To pen up a dog like that is a sin. It would have broken his heart. The will to live would have slowly left his body."

2. "It is very unusual for a hound to be traveling all alone."

3. The narrator believed that the dog was going home to the master he loved.

4. Answers will vary, but should include the fact that the cups probably brought back memories of the narrator's dogs and a contest they were involved in when he was a boy.

Chapter Two: Comprehension and Discussion Questions (Answers may vary.)

1. His mother was part Cherokee.

2. He didn't have any spare money to buy the hound and he could get a collie pup for free. Billy was unappreciative. He insisted on having two hound pups.

3. Although it took Billy's mind off the hounds for a while, when the newness of the traps wore off, he again started pestering about getting the hounds. He really wanted to hunt raccoons, and raccoons were too smart to catch with his traps. Also, although he was very proud of the small animals he caught, he also caught his mother's cat and prize hen.

4. Answers will vary.

Chapter Three: Comprehension and Discussion Questions (Answers may vary.)

1. He found a magazine advertising the sale of redbone coon pups.

2. He sold bait and food to the fishermen. He picked berries and sold them to his grandfather. He sold the hides he got from trapping.

3. Grandpa knew that Billy's dad needed money to buy a mule and he didn't want him to use Billy's money. He said, "Son, it's your money. You worked for it." Later he said, "I don't think. . .I'd let your Pa know. . . .I happen to know he wants to buy that red mule. . . ."

4. Answers will vary, but should include terms such as determined, persevering, hard-working, and religious.

Chapter Four: Comprehension and Discussion Questions (Answers may vary.)

1. The price of the dogs had dropped. The ten dollars was Billy's change.

2. He saw his full reflection for the first time in his life. He realized that he looked a little odd because his hair was wind-blown and he had no comb to fix it.

3. Billy had never seen a school. His mother taught him at home.

4. Answers will vary.

Chapters Five and Six: Vocabulary

1. cautious
2. iodine
3. muster
4. hampered
5. gawked
6. chuckling
7. bawl
8. shucks
9. sober
10. trance
11. querying
12. ventured
13. prowled
14. mumbling

Chapter Five: Comprehension and Discussion Questions (Answers may vary.)

1. Answers will vary, but he was protecting his dog.

2. He had been afraid of marshals because of stories he had heard. Now that the marshal had shown such kindness, he no longer felt that way.

3. The boy dog was larger and was a deeper color red. His chest was broad and solid. He was bold and aggressive. The girl dog was smaller and more timid. She had a small, delicate head. She was smarter and more cautious than the boy dog. Both showed courage when facing the mountain lion.

4. Answers will vary.

Chapter Six: Comprehension and Discussion Questions (Answers may vary)

1. He was trying to decide what to say to his parents about the pups.

2. The names were carved in the bark of a white sycamore tree. The name Dan was large and bold. The name Ann was small and neat.

3. His father and mother said that he should have told them what he was going to do because they had worried; however, they didn't seem angry. His sisters were delighted.

4. Answers will vary.

Chapters Seven and Eight: Vocabulary

1. F	4. M	7. H	10. B	13. C	16. G
2. E	5. K	8. P	11. D	14. N	17. J
3. R	6. A	9. O	12. Q	15. I	18. L

Chapter Seven: Comprehension and Discussion Questions (Answers may vary.)

1. Once a raccoon wraps its paws around something, it won't let go. That makes the paw larger and more difficult to get out of the small space.

2. He tried to climb on the log and get to the coon. Even after Little Ann saved him, he tried to get to it.

3. With the dogs, the raccoons had a sporting chance. With the traps, they had no chance at all.

4. Billy took the hide of the trapped raccoon and scented a trail all over the woods—up trees, on fences, etc.—for his pups to follow. He tried to spread the scent wherever a coon might really go if being hunted.

Chapter Eight: Comprehension and Discussion Questions (Answers may vary.)

1. He cleaned and filled his lantern, he greased his boots, and he sharpened his ax.

2. His father wasn't treating him like a child anymore. He had begun to speak to him like a man.

3. Billy had spoken to the dogs the night before, explaining how important this was to him and telling them to do their best. The next morning the dogs were sitting on the steps, waiting for Billy.

4. Papa had made him feel proud and grown-up. He had called him a man: "If a man's word isn't any good, he's no good himself." A lot of the frustration he had felt disappeared, and the job seemed less overwhelming.

Chapter Nine: Comprehension and Discussion Questions (Answers may vary.)

1. His strength was gone and he believed he would have to give up his attempt to fell the tree.

2. They would build a scarecrow to fool the coon into thinking a man was there. Billy knew Grandpa was serious because of the serious look on his face.

3. He had to fell the tree to get to the coon. Billy believed that he would be letting down his dogs if he gave up. At the same time, he felt badly about cutting down the tree that had been such an important part of his life.

4. He prayed to God to give him strength to finish the job. In Chapter One Billy (as a man) said with the help of God the hound would find its way home to its master. In Chapter Three Billy said, "I decided I'd ask God to help me. . . . I asked God to help me get two hound pups." He also said, "I knew He had helped, for He had given me the heart, courage, and determination."

Chapter Ten: Comprehension and Discussion Questions (Answers may vary.)

1. He quieted them by suggesting that they go inside to see who had the most hides.

2. The hides from the coons he hunted would bring the family much needed money.

3. At one time he had been caught in a trap and had managed to escape. He had learned from this experience.

4. Old Dan figured out that he had to climb up the hollow of the tree. Little Ann opened a hole in the muskrat den for Old Dan.

Chapters Eleven and Twelve: Vocabulary

1. F	4. B	7. D	10. A	13. G	16. I
2. J	5. H	8. E	11. N	14. P	17. M
3. L	6. O	9. K	12. Q	15. R	18. C

Chapter Eleven: Comprehension and Discussion Questions (Answers may vary.)

1. Cons: It was dangerous: there was no moon out; it was foggy; and the snow was slick. Also, his parents warned him not to go. Pros: Ringtails would be hungry and stirring because they had been cooped up during the storm. His lantern light was good. He had made two leather pouches to cover the blades of his ax.

2. He heard Old's Dan's cry for help. Old Dan came to him with his tail between his legs and his head bowed down. Little Ann had fallen into the icy water. She was in danger of freezing to death.

3. Billy had prayed for a message from God telling him what to do. When he heard the metallic sound of the lantern handle hitting the metal frame, it gave him an idea. He took this as being his "miracle instructions." He made a hook on the end of the wire handle and tied it to his pole. He then used it to fish out Little Ann.

4. Answers will vary.

Chapter Twelve: Comprehension and Discussion Questions (Answers may vary.)

1. Answers will vary, but it was likely because they boys were taunting Billy. Also, Rainie had called Grandpa crooked.

2. Rubin was large and husky. He was quiet. He had mean-looking eyes and a rugged face. Rainie was about Billy's age. He was very mean and, therefore, not well liked. He was often the cause of trouble. Rainie always wanted to bet on something. He was rather dirty. According to Billy's mother, Rainie was often beaten by older siblings. Also, they didn't learn any values from their family of thieves. Rumor even had it that their father had killed a man.

3. "He just runs hounds long enough to get them all warmed up, then climbs a tree and disappears."

4. Answers will vary, but probably it was not in the tree because Little Ann never barked treed.

Chapters Thirteen and Fourteen: Vocabulary

1. rope	4. felt malicious delight	7. with a leg on each side	10. repressed
2. monotonous	5. serious	8. uttered impulsively	11. opposition
3. joyful	6. disturbance	9. biting	12. being

Chapter Thirteen: Comprehension and Discussion Questions (Answers may vary.)

1. Billy refused to kill the "ghost coon."

2. Billy's grandfather had threatened to have the boys put in jail if they harmed Billy. Rubin wanted to scare Billy so that he wouldn't tell his grandfather about the money or the threats.

3. Their dog, Old Blue, had provoked a fight with Old Dan. Little Ann came to Old Dan's assistance and the two were beating him. Rubin ran after Billy's dogs with Billy's ax and tripped. He fell on the blade, and it killed him.

4. Billy had wanted to do something to help the Pritchards, but they didn't like to have outsiders around. Putting flowers on the grave made him feel like he was doing something.

Chapter Fourteen: Comprehension and Discussion Questions (Answers may vary.)

1. Grandpa thought it was his fault because he was the one who had suggested that they take the bet.

2. He wanted to discuss the Championship Hunt.

3. Grandpa was trying to stay calm, but he couldn't hold back his emotions. He was going along on an even keel, and then his pent-up emotions broke loose. The comparison was to a car that is riding smoothly and then suddenly goes out of gear.

4. Billy had thought that he would never be able to use the ax again—that it would remind him of Rubin's accident.

Chapter Fifteen: Comprehension and Discussion Questions (Answers may vary.)

1. Their devotion to each other was very unusual. Old Dan wouldn't eat until he was sure Little Ann had her meal too. Old Dan brought the biscuits to Little Ann and gave her one before eating his. Their devotion to Billy was also unusual.

2. He poured him a cup of coffee, which he had never been allowed to drink at home.

3. There was a superstition that if you heard more than one screech owl, it meant bad luck. Billy tried to convince himself, therefore, that he had heard the same owl from two different trees.

4. Billy cried for joy when Little Ann won a silver cup for being the best-looking hound.

Chapter Sixteen: Comprehension and Discussion Questions (Answers may vary.)

1. The judge couldn't figure out how Little Ann had discovered the coon on the tall sycamore tree.

2. They needed one more coon to tie.

3. Answers will vary, but probably will include the following: Billy was very young to have trained his dogs so well. They probably admired Billy's determination and his dogs' devotion to him and to each other.

4. Little Ann slept as close to Old Dan as she could. Little Ann pulled the coon off Old Dan's head. They each licked the other's cuts and bleeding ears.

Chapter Seventeen: Comprehension and Discussion Questions (Answers may vary.)

1. Billy convinced Papa that Old Dan would not give up. "He'd die before he'd leave a coon in a tree." Answers will vary as to Papa's decision, but he probably knew that Billy would not leave his dogs stranded and wouldn't want to leave Billy alone in such a dangerous situation.

2. He asked Papa to shoot the gun in the air. He thought Little Ann might leave the coon to come to him, and she did.

3. Grandpa had fallen face down in the icy sleet. His right foot became wedged in the fork of a broken tree limb. He twisted his ankle so badly that the pain made him unconcious.

4. They ran in the direction of the coon as if reading Billy's mind. It surprised the judge because hounds weren't usually that smart.

Chapter Eighteen: Comprehension and Discussion Questions (Answers may vary)

1. One of the best doctors in Texas was in the camp.

2. When Mr. Benson said that the dogs were frozen solid, Billy thought that the dogs were dead.

3. They were kind, supportive, and helpful. When Mr. Benson frightened Billy, he was sorry. They helped go after the dogs. They warmed the dogs with "their gentle hands." When Billy won, "there was a roar of approval from the crowd."

4. He knew that his little sister would be expecting the cup.

Chapters Nineteen and Twenty: Vocabulary

1. bellow	4. foliage	7. ghastly	10. sandstone	13. predatory
2. entrails	5. vibration	8. ledge	11. sacred	
3. fangs	6. gristle	9. pitiful	12. peroxide	

Billy loves Little Ann and Old Dan.

Chapter Nineteen: Comprehension and Discussion Questions (Answers may vary.)

1. "In his veins flowed the breeded blood of a hunting hound. In his heart there was no fear."

2. Billy hacked at the mountain lion with the cutting blade of a double-bitted ax. The dogs got between the mountain lion and Billy. They "took the ripping, slashing claws" meant for Billy.

3. It was beautiful. From there you could see the river and the trees and hear the voices of the hounds.

4. The money earned from the Championship Hunt gave them enough to move into town where her children could get an education.

Chapter Twenty: Comprehension and Discussion Questions (Answers may vary.)

1. To Billy's surprise, everyone was in very good spirits. Mama and the girls were laughing and joking. Papa no longer had a defeated look on his face; he was very happy.

2. There was an old Indian legend about a little boy and girl who froze to death during a blizzard. When their bodies were found in the spring, a beautiful red fern had grown between their bodies. The legend went on to tell that only an angel could plant the seeds of a red fern, and that the spot on which one grew was sacred.

3. Answers will vary.

4. Answers will vary.

Spotlight Literary Skill: Mood

1. anger   2. surprise   3. fear; frustration   4. suspense; fear   5. happiness

Spotlight Literary Skill: Cause and Effect

1. C	3. I	5. H	7. F	9. E
2. A	4. B	6. J	8. D	10. G

Spotlight Literary Skill: Colorful Language (Answers may vary.)

The following are a few examples of similes: [The cup] sparkled like a white star. (p.6) I . . . was as thin as a bean pole. (p.15) The lawns. . .looked like green carpets. (p.30) The words. . .sounded like the squeaky old pulley. (p.36) The starlit heaven reminded me of a large blue umbrella. (p. 72) Tall sycamores gleamed like white streamers. (p.72) [The big tree] was like a king in his own domain. (p. 77) Grandpa flew out of gear like an old Model-T Ford. (p.157) Grandpa roared like a bear. (p. 205) [The dogs] looked like white ghosts. (p. 211)

The following are a few examples of personification: I set out to trap Mister Ringtail. (p. 55) A big grinning Ozark moon. . . (p. 72) [The tree] was like a king. . . . (p.77) The wind. . .seemed to be angry. (p. 94) "I'm sorry, [tree]. . .I hope you understand. (p. 96) "Thanks, old lantern. . . ." (p. 121) [The cold water] seemed to be angry. (p. 121) Tall stalks of cane were weaving and dancing. (p. 202) The summer breeze. . .hummed a tune. (p. 247) The red fern. . .danced to the music of the hills. (p. 247) NOTE: pages may vary according to the edition of the book you are reading.

Crossword Puzzle: